LIBRARY OF AWESOME ANIMALS

JAPANESE SPIDER CRAB

By Catherine C. Finan

Consultant: Darin Collins, DVM
Director, Animal Health Programs, Woodland Park Zoo

BEARPORT PUBLISHING

Minneapolis, Minnesota

Credits

cover, © Jane Rix/Alamy; 3, © LELACHANOK/Shutterstock; 4, 5, © pr2is/Shutterstock; 7, © Urs Flueeler/EyeEm/ Getty Images; 8, © slowmotiongli/Shutterstock; 9, © Leonid Serebrennikov/Alamy Stock Photo; 11, © slowmotiongli/Shutterstock; 12, © Scenics & Science/Alamy Stock Photo; 13, © Christian Siegenthaler/ Shutterstock; 15, © Engdao Wichitpunya/Alamy Stock Photo; 16, © oksana2010/Shutterstock; 17, © GOLFX/iStock; 18, © Konstantin Novikov/Shutterstock; 19, © Arunee Rodloy/Shutterstock; 21, © f11photo/Shutterstock; 23, © Kiwisoul/Shutterstock

President: Jen Jenson
Director of Product Development: Spencer Brinker
Editor: Allison Juda
Designer: Micah Edel

Library of Congress Cataloging-in-Publication Data

Names: Finan, Catherine C., 1972- author.
Title: Japanese spider crab / Catherine C. Finan.
Description: Minneapolis, Minnesota : Bearport Publishing Company, [2021] | Series: Library of awesome animals | Includes bibliographical references and index.
Identifiers: LCCN 2020008955 (print) | LCCN 2020008956 (ebook) | ISBN 9781647471439 (library binding) | ISBN 9781647471545 (paperback) | ISBN 9781647471651 (ebook)
Subjects: LCSH: Spider crabs—Juvenile literature.
Classification: LCC QL444.M33 F56 2021 (print) | LCC QL444.M33 (ebook) | DDC 595.3/84—dc23
LC record available at https://lccn.loc.gov/2020008955
LC ebook record available at https://lccn.loc.gov/2020008956

For more information, write to Bearport Publishing, 5357 Penn Avenue South, Minneapolis, MN 55419.
Printed in the United States of America.

Contents

AWESOME Japanese Spider Crabs!

SNAP! A Japanese spider crab pinches its strong claws. A monster feeder of the deep ocean floor, the Japanese spider crab is awesome!

THE JAPANESE SPIDER CRAB GOT ITS NAME BECAUSE IT LOOKS LIKE A SPIDER!

World's Largest Crab

The Japanese spider crab is the largest known crab on Earth. It can have a **leg span** of over 12 feet (3.7 m). That's about the same as the height of an adult elephant!

These crabs can weigh about 40 pounds (18.1 kg) when fully grown. That's heavy for a crab, but it's light for such a giant creature!

MALE JAPANESE SPIDER CRABS GROW LARGER THAN FEMALE CRABS.

Crazy Crab Bodies

Japanese spider crabs have eight legs—like spiders! Plus, they have two feeding arms that can grow even longer than their legs. Each long arm ends in a huge claw. **YIKES!**

The crab's oval-shaped body is covered in a hard, bumpy shell. Little crabby eyes are found on short **stalks** at the front of its body.

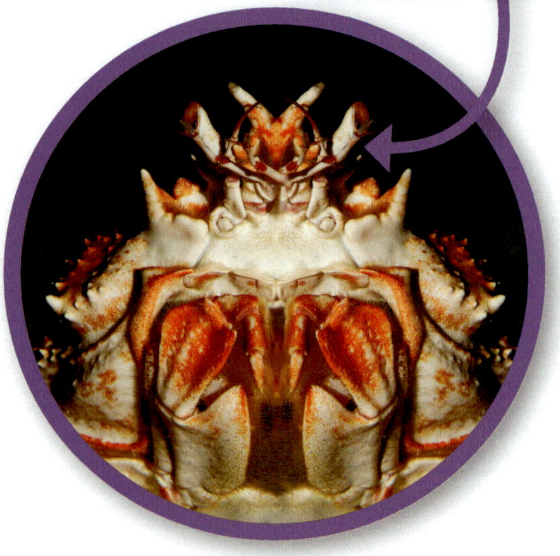

An eye stalk

THE JAPANESE SPIDER CRAB'S BODY IS SMALL COMPARED TO ITS LEGS. IT GROWS TO JUST 15 INCHES (38.1 CM) LONG.

A Deep, Dark Home

These giant crabs may sound scary, but chances are good you'll never run into one! Japanese spider crabs live deep in the Pacific Ocean near Japan—really deep. They're found at the ocean bottom, usually between 500 and 1,000 ft (150 and 300 m) down. There, the water is dark and cold. They only come to warmer, **shallower** water to **mate** in the spring.

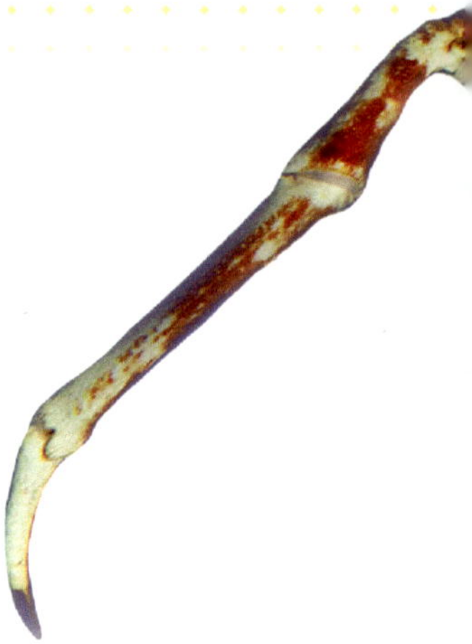

IN JAPAN, IT'S AGAINST THE LAW TO CATCH JAPANESE SPIDER CRABS DURING THEIR MATING SEASON.

Tiny Crab Babies

After mating, the female crab can lay over one million eggs! The mother carries the eggs on her body. How does she fit them all? Each egg is smaller than a grain of sand!

Few of the eggs **survive**. The crab babies that do **hatch** don't look anything like their giant parents. They're more like tiny, see-through aliens! **CRAZY!**

A newly hatched Japanese spider crab

IT TAKES ABOUT 70 DAYS FOR THE BABIES TO START TO LOOK LIKE TINY CRABS.

A young Japanese spider crab

A Long, Long Life

As the crabs get older, they grow larger. And they have plenty of time to grow. Japanese spider crabs can live for up to 100 years.

But their long lives aren't easy. Most Japanese spider crabs lose at least one leg to fishing nets or hungry **predators**. Sometimes they grow another leg to replace the first. That's awesome!

THESE CRABS HAVE BEEN KNOWN TO SURVIVE WITH UP TO THREE MISSING LEGS!

A missing leg

I'll Eat Anything!

Japanese spider crabs aren't picky eaters. They will chow down on just about anything smaller than they are! What's on the menu? The crabs eat **algae**, ocean plants, fish, and **shellfish**.

While they look like scary hunters, Japanese spider crabs are anything but! They usually make an easy meal of animals that are already dead! **YUM!**

JAPANESE SPIDER CRABS USE THEIR STRONG CLAWS TO OPEN SHELLFISH.

Hide-and-Seek

Because of their huge size, Japanese spider crabs don't have many predators. But they do have to steer clear of hungry octopuses!

These clever crabs have tricks that keep them hidden, which keeps them safe. They have bumpy, spotted bodies, and some younger crabs cover their shells with seaweed and small sea animals. This helps them blend in with the ocean floor.

An octopus

A decorator crab sticks plants to its body.

JAPANESE SPIDER CRABS ARE A KIND OF **DECORATOR** CRAB. THESE CRABS COVER THEIR SHELLS FOR **CAMOUFLAGE**.

A Killer Crab?

Japanese spider crabs are huge and look freaky, but are they deadly? One story about the crabs says they drag sailors off boats and eat them. ***EEK!*** Could it be true?

You wouldn't want to get too close to their huge claws. And they would feed on people who have drowned. But these gentle giants won't hurt you if you leave them alone! That's awesome!

JAPANESE SPIDER CRABS HAVE EARNED THE NICKNAME DEAD MAN'S CRAB, BUT THEY DON'T KILL HUMANS!

Information Station

JAPANESE SPIDER CRABS ARE AWESOME!

LET'S LEARN EVEN MORE ABOUT THEM.

Kind of animal: The Japanese spider crab is an arthropod (AHR-thruh-*pahd*). An arthropod has jointed limbs, a body made up of segments, an **exoskeleton**, and no backbone.

Other arthropods: Insects, crabs, lobsters, and spiders are all arthropods!

Size: Japanese spider crabs have a leg span of 12 ft (3.7 m). That's about as long as a small car!

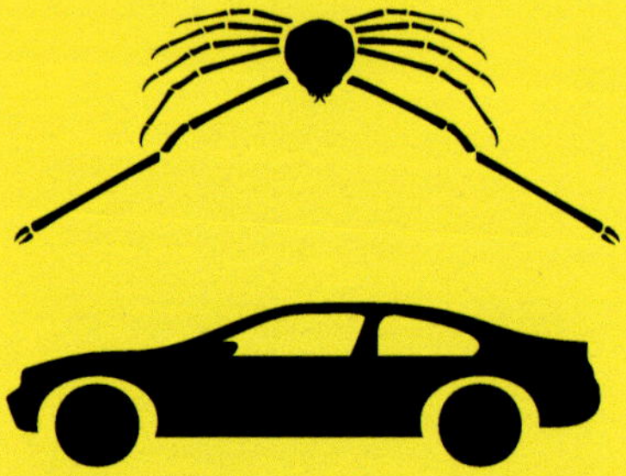

JAPANESE SPIDER CRABS AROUND THE WORLD

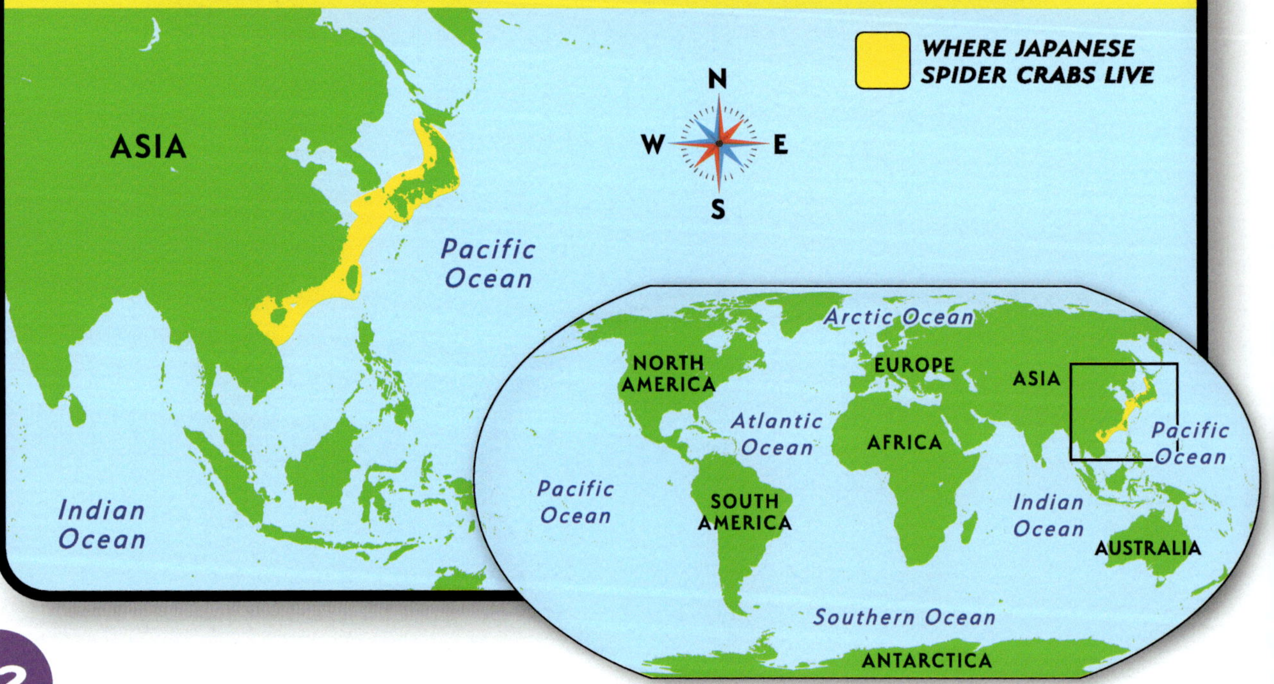

Glossary

algae tiny plantlike living things that grow in or near water

camouflage a way of hiding something by covering or coloring it so it looks like its surroundings

decorator one who changes the way something looks by adding decorations

exoskeleton an outer supporting structure, such as the shell of a crab

hatch to come out of an egg

leg span the distance from the tip of one leg to the tip of another leg

mate to come together to have young

predators animals that hunt and kill other animals for food

shallower not as deep

shellfish sea creatures with a shell; crabs, lobsters, shrimp, and clams are all shellfish

stalks thin connecting parts

survive to stay alive

Index

Read More

Bassier, Emma. *Japanese Spider Crabs (Weird and Wonderful Animals)*. Minneapolis: Pop! (2019).

Bodden, Valerie. *Crabs (Amazing Animals)*. Mankato, MN: Creative Education (2017).

Perkins, Wendy. *Japanese Spider Crabs (Weird and Unusual Animals)*. Mankato, MN: Amicus Ink (2018).

Learn More Online

1. Go to **www.factsurfer.com**
2. Enter "**Spider Crab**" into the search box.
3. Click on the cover of this book to see a list of websites.

About the Author

Catherine C. Finan is a nature lover living in northeastern Pennsylvania. One of her favorite things to do is visit aquariums, where she is always on the lookout for awesome Japanese spider crabs!